The Five Mile Press

SWEET
(non-Monday)
DREAMS

In The Mood For Food

I THINK
NOT!

ASSUME THE
ATTITUDE

NOPE. NOT WORKING.

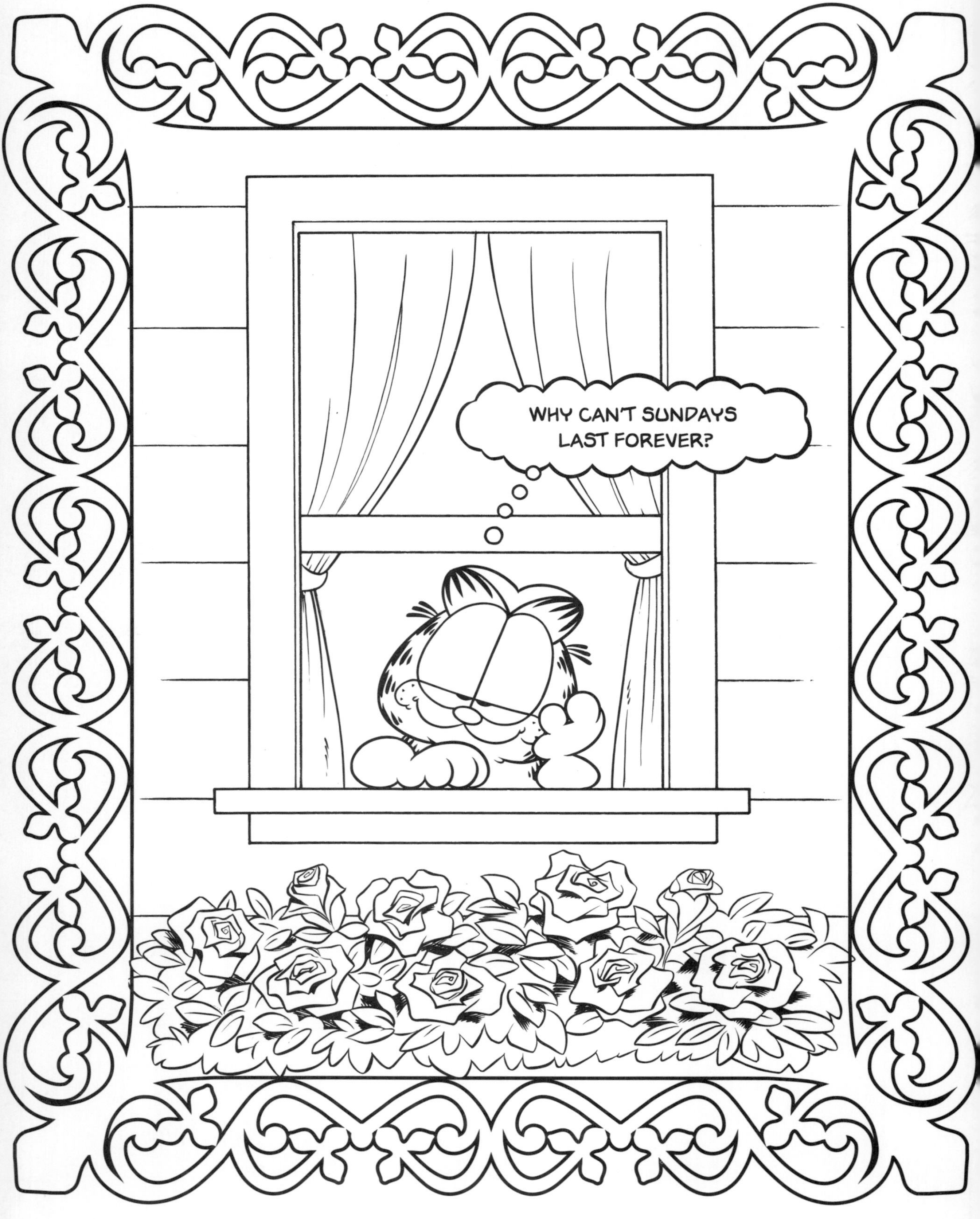
WHY CAN'T SUNDAYS
LAST FOREVER?

ASK ME
IF I CARE

NOT GOING ANYWHERE
NOW MORE FAT
CHIPS
TV
PIZZA

COME AT ME, MONDAY

Gone Fishing

HOLIDAY DREAMING ...

Food Helps!

TOO COOL FOR MONDAY

ANTI-MONDAY
MUSKETEERS

BOYCOTT MONDAY
ODIE
&
GFLD1

Holiday Dreaming ...

THAT
END-OF-THE-WEEK
FEELING

THE WEEKEND!

Group Hug
TO GET THROUGH MONDAY

KA-WANGA!

HOLIDAY
DREAMING...

CHALLENGE ACCEPTED

WOULDN'T YOU
RATHER BE HERE?

WATCH OUT!
MONDAY'S COMING

IT'S A JUNGLE

WEDGIE
TIME!

BOO!

COOL BANANAS

MONDAY...
PFFFT

MONDAY
MONDAY
MONDAY
MONDAY
MONDAY
MONDAY
MONDAY

I HATE MONDAYS

YOU AGAIN

ZZZ
ZZZ
ZZZ
ZZZZ

MONDAY
GRRR
MONDAY
GRRR
MONDAY
GRRR

AN APPLE A DAY KEEPS THE MONDAY AWAY

ENOUGH COLOURING ... BRING ME LASAGNE